SOB
Copyright © 2011 by Loria Taylor.

Sibling Rivalry Press, LLC
13913 Magnolia Glen Drive
Alexander, AR 72002

www.siblingrivalrypress.com

Library of Congress Control Number: 2011929927

ISBN: 978-0-9832931-7-0

First Sibling Rivalry Press Edition, August 2011.

"Patio Gas Can" was published by *Breadcrumb Scabs*. Gratitude to editor Lena Judith Drake.

"A Divination" and "Surely" were published at *vox poetica*. Gratitude to editor Annmarie Lockhart.

SOB

LORIA TAYLOR

Sibling Rivalry Press

Look here
Only you could bring yourself down into this
River of tears, of bitter pain, and finally of numbness
If you could only see yourself
As you truly are, then perhaps you'd bloom finally or die for sure.

CONTENTS

SOB

WINTER BIRTH

It's true I was born
To a frozen ground
Cold Mother
Chill of a Winter Birth
Bone dry and dreary
Bone ache and weary
It's true I was borne
Of ice and tombs
Static disease solid underneath
Chill of a Winter's Curse
Bone dry and dreary
Bone ache, weary

It's true
I was born
Cold Mother

TIMELINES OF DYING WOMEN

Subject 1:

Her brother dies a few months earlier
so Pandora's Box is opened,
and my mother,
her brothers and sisters
will be picked off now,
one by one. Dead.

She gets cancer.
She fights cancer.
Cancer goes away.

Cancer comes back.
With a vengeance.

Life recedes.
Her only treatment options
are to do nothing or basically bring her
to the brink of death
so she can live.

Chemo.
Kills off her entire immune system.
Almost kills her off.

Transplant.
Infection.
Compromised breathing.

ICU.
Back to regular ward.
Half a good day.
Many bad days.

Moved to "step under ICU" ward.
ICU again.
...and repeat until dead.

Subject 2:

Woman is born.

The doctors think she might have a heart
murmur. She doesn't.

She has tendencies
toward negative thinking.

She is clumsy.
She faints. A lot.
She likes to think of death.

She turns 30.

She watches Subject 1.
She eats a high-fiber chocolate granola bar.
At some point afterward,

she dies.

NEW GUY

The new one says
casually
I like you.
I say, I like you, too.
We continue driving
barely touching fingers.
That new one
with his easy smile
that I sense is not so easy.
The new one
who will never win my complete adoration.
Typical manspeak, he meant it as a compliment.
It wasn't.
He said
I like hanging out with you
and that is the same as saying
fuck you.

DEFINITIONS

Permafunk. The experience of being in a depressive state long after it's fashionable.

Major Depression. Depression that is major in its intensity. See also permafunk.

Darkened rooms. Heaven. See also music-for-the-soul.

Openness. The action of sufficiently masking that you're not really there, you are nothing, you don't exist.

Music-for-the-Soul. Coldplay. The truest thing he ever said. See also confusion.

Confusion. Furrow-browed disorientation. How can one song resonate for him and for me when we're so far apart?

The Inevitability of Truth. After you remove the first layer, after you remove the despair, you can feel a more profound, objective level of hopelessness. The pure absence of hope. Nothing to get upset about.

Bare bones. Absence of self.

Glass house. Next time you see me, look closer.

A DIVINATION

a divination of the signs a Thursday night
road unsafe under water, road unsafe regardless
slower traffic right lane, fast forward left lane
I drive on the shoulder
mile marker 103
three men, one love
construction ahead
fines double when workers are present
fines double when hope is present
there are places on Arkansas roadways
that if you had a flat tire
you'd never know for all the potholes
it feels the same, the road and the trouble
the road and the mechanism
never has the future been so transparent

THE WHITE KIND

When I was 18, I could easily take naps
There was nothing to sleep
Nothing to stretching out on the couch with the blue afghan
my aunt made in the 90's

At 22, I could drift off
But with requirements
A dark room, silence from the neighbor upstairs

At 28, benadryl
Was the only way to sleep
Though rest has always been hard to come by

At 31, almost 32,
A cocktail of benadryl and ambien,
Endearingly called bambien by those in the know, puts me
to sleep
But only with the minty green application of icy hot to my
tight muscles
A mask to block the intrusion of light
And ear plugs to eliminate all noise, even the white kind

IT'S EARLY YET

I remember so many things he said
Words with prickly edges that sometimes still stick in my
skin and mind
Don't be such a silly girl
Don't take this the wrong way, you're easy, you're simple
I'm just being honest
I have no affection to give you how can you hate or blame
me for that is it all or nothing with you have a good day

I remember so many things you said
Words profound but with a sister-friend shelter over me
Don't torture yourself
Did it ever occur to you that you ruined a song for him?
Let's go get you some pizza and a coke, how about a cookie?
Girl please

SINCE THE DAY I WAS BORN

it's a rumor
of life-threatening proportions

mothers, grandmothers, aunts
all dying
since the day I was born

my mother was someone else's mother
long before she was mine
and I used to wonder if I'd die too

this story ends
life
as a life-threatening condition

FAMILY PORTRAIT, CIRCA 2006

Last fall, my father, grandmother and I
visited the graveyards
of loved ones long gone
her mother, my father's grandmother
cousins, brothers never known
beneath the soil
the leaves, they were bright
red, yellow, some were green or brown
framed the headstones
and the three of us,
a family portrait

AMATEUR

He says he wants a picture of me,
not just any picture of me.
I wonder if I can hire a photographer
to make me look appropriately buxom
but also amateur
so he'll think it's no effort at all for me to look sexy.
There are just so few flattering angles in the world.
It's akin to disguising
a poem
as a sentence
or pretending a significant work of art
is as easy as the pie you'll never bake.

FAILING

my heart is going
slowly now
it gave a good go of it
beating and all
those moments of bitter retreat
ebb and flow of blood
coming in and out of spite
until
slowly now
the organ is engorged
swollen, dying of itself
pumping painfully
ruefully spasming
giving a good go of it
slowly now

HOARDING DISTORTIONS

Never, ever
is a distortion
Always, forever
is a distortion
Magnifying
is a distortion
Minimizing
is a distortion
Hording hurts
is a distortion
Denying gifts or pleasure
is a distortion
Reasoning with my emotions
is a distortion
I want to die
is a distortion
I want to live
is a distortion
all of it
all the thoughts I have
the heart that beats in my chest
the mind that races constantly
without mercy
is a distortion

TO MY DEAREST

To my dearest.
Or reasonable facsimile.

When I look into your brown eyes
I can't help but notice
you have a few stray hairs between your eyebrows
not an unibrow exactly
but I'd like to pluck them just the same.

To my dearest.

You are quite short
being less than a foot taller than me
I have strict height standards
still you've wooed me with talk of your serial killer
tendencies.

To my dearest.

My
you have quite a bit of chest hair
I see
but that jawline is killer
and I wonder what you might be like
if I could get past your issues.

To my dearest.

You have left me
but you are very cute
I thought the crotch shot was particularly attractive
if not a bit suggestive
but I fear you are a conservative sort.

To my dearest.

Whoever you are
know I will love you despite your transgressions
and allow you
to trample me to your error-ridden
and flawed heart's content.

DELICIOUS

I do not cut
I pick
skin ripped
away
searing, acute pain
good, feels right
feels like home
a moment of focused hurt
a magnifying glass raised
to the sun and directed
on me
burning
deliciously

THE BITTER END

And so we're here, my friend says drunkenly.
The bitter end.

I've been living here for ages, I say in a sleep haze.

We talk for a few moments. We slur. It doesn't matter how
indecipherable the words are. We understand each other.

I think I drift off to sleep. He's talking to other people at the
bar. He tells me tips on dating that we both forget almost
instantly.

Did I tell you about the dream I had the other night? The
one about the woman who said my credit card was rejected
and judged me harshly when I asked her to run it again,
that there must be a mistake? I ask.

Ooooh-we-oooh I look just like Buddy Holly, oh-oh and
you're Mary Tyler Moore, he sings over me.

I mean to shrug my shoulders, but instead I fall asleep
again.

NOVA OF US

What is a speck in the night sky
a meaningless dot to those below
is significant in space
You and everyone else
watched our star explode from the Green Earth
while I was captured by the gravitational pull of our
destruction
and forced to endure an endless orbit
around the nova of us

WE'VE DECIDED TO MAX OUT THE PROZAC

What has come about is that I think my relationships with men are doomed to fail. It is a belief, something that feels real and true and absolute. I don't know how to combat it. Once I make a date to meet a man, it starts a countdown to the end of our relationship. I literally hear the clock ticking. A good friend of mine said, *you've been put through the ringer, don't be so hard on yourself.* Another said, *don't make other men pay for what's been done to you.*

One theory is, in some ways, I *chose* my previous relationship *because* he was obviously flawed, so I didn't have to wonder what was going to go wrong. That feels both true and not-completely-true. If one relationship, one that by all accounts was not good for me, if that one relationship can create so much sorrow, can spiral me this far down, how am I ever going to survive dating? Was it coincidence? That this dysfunctional relationship and breakup simply corresponded and exacerbated a depressive episode I would have had anyway? I want someone to tell me I'm not weak.

I'm so tired of ambivalence.

BEFORE WHAT CAME AFTER

I felt sure
what I felt
was real
That Carolina held me close
A home idolized
idealized
And then a realization
stark reality
of exile
betrayal
And too
he was Carolina
he didn't keep me
either
For a time
happiness and home
before what came after

LOST

I liked how his hands felt on my back
when we were hugging or fucking
The last time
He took my face in his hands
and kissed me softly
It was a display of tenderness that was not lost on me
In the middle of the night
I'd drift toward consciousness
to the weight of his hand on me
heavy and sweet
I usually held his face in my hands
a tactile substitute for gazing in his eyes
The last time
He took my face in his hands
and kissed me softly
Now I see
it was a wave goodbye that was lost on me

MANTRA

If you call
you're just like him
If you don't call
you're just like him
If you call but not in a timely manner
you're just like him
If you're tall
you're just like him
If you have a decent sense of humor
you're just like him
If you are a permanent bachelor
you're just like him
If you say you love the way I feel in your arms
you're just like him
If you're looking for someone to kill time with
you're just like him
If you will never have affection for me
you're just like him
If you give mixed signals
you're just like him
If you're selfish
you're just like him
Even if your name is different
you're just like him
Even if they say you're not
you're just like him
Even if I try to give you a chance
you're just like him

LEAVING: A GOODBYE FOR HER GOING

I can feel her leaving
silently exiting
in contrast
with her violent entrance.
Pain is the fountain of youth
where my disappointments
my punishments
bring me
back
to day one.
I dreamed of thawing light
and now that it's here
the words and the gift
she gave
are dissipating
and I'm sad to see them go.

MILK

I think the milk is going bad
can't quite make out the expiration date
I'll only know if it's gone bad for sure after the fact

Sometimes when the milk is going south
it stinks up the whole refrigerator or in any case
something is funny about it but not in a good way

Your milk will spoil
inevitably
I wonder if it's partly my fault
did I leave the jug out of the refrigerator too long
have I sped up the spoiling

Or was it bad before it ever got to me
Was it bad in the first place
Your milk won't divulge its secrets
I have to figure it out on my own
Your origins, your past

Sometimes it takes a few days
to notice something is not right
Sometimes sour milk doesn't taste sour
Or my sense of smell is off
Sometimes I am too thirsty to care if it's good or bad
Sometimes I don't even try to tell the difference
I drink

Remember
once the milk goes bad
there's no going back

I don't even like milk that much but I'm a woman

PHOTOGRAPHERS OF MY DAYS

What slashes through my veins
the blade parallel to my arm
not perpendicular
the right way
is that I will leave no trace on your life.

The first one
he wasn't a picture taker
but six months and he never wanted to capture me
for all time
One day
I saw his screensaver
and what must have been his ex-girlfriend and her child
flashing across the screen.

And then you
pictures of everything in digital
so much so that clicking *becomes*
your version of living
you don't bother
with me.

UNFINISHED: THE HAIKUS

fingers through your hair
the feel of just-mown lawn grass
sparks fly with my touch

so you want to go back
Japan is lovely I hear
no more me to see

COUGAR

younger men
represent the trivial
the unburdened and underbaggaged

slips of thought
mainly instinct
no wondering about the formation of scar tissue
yet
a blank canvas
waiting
for me to do the scarring

THE BRUSH OFF

he planted me
in sickly soil
but I survived
now where you watered me
the skin is turning brown
flakes of you repel against the stalk of me
you are a scab
no longer attached
ready to be brushed off

ON HAPPY BIRTHDAYS

My birthday is January 2nd.
My aunt Celia's birthday is January 3rd.
My aunt Tywanua's birthday is January 4th.
Tywanua is dead.
Safe to say Celia is dying and will be dead soon.
Cancer, you know, kills.
Kills people dead.
Kills people with January 3rd and 4th birthdays.
I do not worry about cancer for January 2nd birthdays
anymore.
I asked my mother everyday when I was 8 if I had cancer.
I asked her if I was going to die.
I am not dead.
All the dying is murder, though.
Tywanua dead.
Celia soon.
Me, not soon enough.

TO C. ROLL

I dreamt of you
under halogen lights
and in busy venues
I dreamt of large chunks of your sweetness
melting in my mouth
I've had you in my mind
so many times
but can never find you in the wilderness of reality
Because I dream of you
Because I don't deny it
I am made a joke
but for your gooeyness
I pray you will continue to make me your fool

THE FUTURE IS ALWAYS TRUNCATED

Yesterday
I talked to the flake.

I told him my father
gave me a tour of the ice storm devastation
in Northeast Arkansas.

Yesterday
I visited my great aunt
who's dead
and her hands looked like plastic
with caked-on makeup.
My mother said she looked much better.

Yesterday
I drove and drove
but when I got home
I didn't take the laundry out of my car.
It's still there
with my Ritz crackers.

Today
I wear bright flowers
and tired eyes
and wait for the day to be over,
8 to 5 and all of it.
I have been rejected by a man who is 6'5
before I ever knew he existed
because on eHarmony one is expected to browse
and close or open each match that is sent to your account,
and for the life of me,
I can't see how rejection is healthy.

Today
I will rest on my haunches and hope for the best.
I might take the laundry out of my car
or I might not.
I might call a friend far away, but who knows.

Tomorrow
The dentist.
Another TB test.
Exercise.
Aunt.

TALKING SWEET TO A SOLDIER

The beauty of talking sweet to a soldier
is when the talk turns bitter
what are they going to do
leave you
War-torn countries make a man need a distraction
I am happy to oblige
I tell myself
the drama is free
no late fees
I'm grateful he takes my mind away
from the war zones of heartache and the frigid temperatures
of my workplace environment
The beauty of talking sweet to a soldier
is he'll take it like a child
and petulantly ask for more

HOW TO GET WHAT YOU WANT: IN MEMORY

She told the nurse,
Leave me alone
I'm trying to die here.
97 and a tiny little thing
97 and feisty as hell
97 and gone on
to wherever it is she wanted to go.

HARDER NOW

it's harder now
the way it goes, the way it blows
wind and moods
uncherished respites
cold lingers in my fingers,
places hidden and outright
the right hand heavier than the left
circulation poor
Pouring
it's harder now
the way it goes, the way it blows

MIAMI

My ex-boyfriend went to Miami for four days in April.
I know because I drove him from the airport.
He went to a strip club.
He took pictures of girls he met there.
One night on the town, three pictures of these girls.
I know because one morning after he'd gone to work,
I looked through the pictures on his camera.
Six months with me, not a one picture did he take.
I know because I was there.
I know because he's so predictable.
I know because I drove him to the airport.

POTENTIAL

I've got potential.
I have plenty of mistakes to make
but instead of making them,
instead of diligently moving toward disaster,

I choose to consider the dog shit in the middle of my floor.

My life is on hold while I wait
to be skinny and attractive enough
to look pretty through tears
while cutting skin tags on my body with rusty scissors.

BETWEEN DEATH AND DECAY

My aunt had cancer.
Actually, she still does.
It's just rotting with her bones in an underground cavern.
Between birth and decay,
it's the suffering that counts.
Malinger away.
Two other aunts have cancer now.
Don't they deserve it, never coming to visit
never seeing the suffering until the end.
More endings coming forthwith.

ON FRIENDLY TERMS

How's this for dirt.

You know about the first time.
No need to reiterate.
The chair was fun.
The couch was okay.
The car had its charm.
The bed was nice.

On my knees was not. Remember how I made you choose
whether you wanted me to give you attention or get your
towel wet by putting it under my knees in the shower
because I was tired of getting bruises. Remember how you
actually paused to consider which would be better or worse.

The best I ever had was on your bathroom counter. The
soap was rattling, unseen objects crashing, as you were
going going going 'til gone. To this day, despite however I
think of you, I am quite fond your bathroom.

The dirtiest thing I ever did was fake it.

The dirtiest thing I ever did was take it.

KILLING MY MOTHER(S)

I don't want to kill my mother. My Aunt Ty died. Now, two other aunts on that same side of the family have cancer. These three aunts have at least one thing in common: they always swore that there'd been a mistake and I was their daughter. My aunts soon to be dead or already so. And I wonder, if I've killed my other mothers, am I going to kill my own mother?

GNAW

My dog had a bone
but no meat on it
not even much of a scent
where there should have been
flavor and bite
My friend nodded saying
it's a shame
puppies having puppies
but she didn't know better
She just wanted a chance
at a real bone
but she has the real thing now
and I give her
bacon-flavored bones everyday

ROLEPLAY

This is me, dealing with myself. It's not about him, she says. She wants you to know this with absolute certainty. *This is a period of self-reflection. This means something,* she says. Her urgency transcends her words. You're not sure what, but there's something you're not getting. You're missing something, or she's missed something. Something is missing. She looks at you as if you're to respond. Say something. Vague alarms go off in your head. She's not quite there, again. She's dramatic, but harmless, *quirky.* She's someone to roll your eyes at, a decent show sometimes. But it can be too much. She can say too much. You can tell she sincerely wants for you to understand but is having a hard time bridging the gap between her broken synapses, between her mind and yours. Having a hard time finding the right combination of words that will transform her gibberish into meaning, something meaningful, to you and to her.

She's having a hard time. She's having an inconvenient time. But there's nothing to be done. As hard as she is trying, you know there's no connecting, there's no talking it out. Rationalizing it. You listen for a few minutes more, maybe 10 minutes, maybe 20. Then, you have to shut her out. Make her stop. After all, she can't stop herself. She is completely incapable of doing that. Really. You're doing her a favor.

HOW TO NAB A MAN

- Do not make him uncomfortable. Men do not like to be uncomfortable.

- Do not allow awkward moments to make the man uncomfortable.

- In the investment-return mindset of the man, putting in effort to avoid awkward moments is a little too much of an effort. He will let you go.

- Never ask for more than a man is currently giving. If you do, this will be awkward.

- Do NOT demand anything of the man in question. This offense is punishable in impenetrable silence.

- Do not complain about basketball or football.

- Pretend not to know as much about any subject as the man. Even if the man is stupid.

- Pretend you do not make more money than the man.

- Smile, for Christ's sake.

- Smile when he tells you appalling things, like how he was at a strip club and a Thai stripper had her, "for lack of a better word," pussy in his face. Pretend the word "vagina" does not exist and pussy is, in fact, a better word.

- Nod reassuringly when he tells you he doesn't think he's going to go through with this drug deal after all.

- It goes without saying, make him feel comfortable at your expense.

- Pretend not to be annoyed if, by the second date, he's already insisting you pay for everything.

- If a man says something insulting to you, make like you haven't heard. If a man continues to insult you, make light of it and yourself. Pride is not more important than causing an awkward moment, now is it?

- You should not have an expectation that a man will ever follow through and call you, see you, think of you when he says he's going to.

- Don't worry your pretty little head. He is not thinking of you right now, but you are to think of him constantly so as to boost his psychic ego.

- Act interested in wrestling.

- Do not insist on watching anything you like.

- Do not be dramatic or show hurt feelings. Awkward.

- Play games. They love games.

- And finally, don't let him know you have him pegged. He's a "mysterious" creature and it will ruin everything.

ENTRAPMENT

So this is simultaneously it
end of him, end of him
the two of them should run off together
bound by their would-be wounded souls
unchained to my inconvenience and instability.
I should give the international one's number
to the local one
both law enforcement sorts
I entrapped them both
sue me.
Or better yet
leave me.

CONTEXTUAL NORMALCY

My friend says
it's perfectly normal
in context

My lip
swelled to the size of Angelina Jolie's lips on collagen
came close to anaphylactic shock
but for severe allergies
it's perfectly normal
in context

I can't concentrate
and I panic often
but for being depressed
it's perfectly normal
in context

I peek around the corner
to see if she's in her office
and feel relief when she's not
but for being paranoid
it's perfectly normal
in context

And I think
I don't want to be in context
if I'm perfectly normal
what fun am I?

WAR HOME

When he comes home
I envision an indeterminable adjustment period
because mortars and murder
are easier for his mind to handle than home
because mental health
is not an appropriate topic until after the fact
because his eyes gleamed
on the plane ride to Afghanistan and died once the bullets
started to whiz by
because he holds it in
war is home now
For his sake, I wonder if he ought to just stay over there

WHAT HE DID

he did what he did
but I still think of him fondly
when I opened the door
I took his breath away
something most unexpected
something so surprising
even to him
to the both of us

PROPER BURIAL

Gone two months, she's been
Gone too long
They buried her in the cheapest coffin they could find
Pastel iridescent pink
An eyesore
Not quite as bad as the tumors that disfigured her body
Turning her from someone they knew into a fright
A freak
Appalling on both counts
I don't blame them for going on the cheap
There wasn't much money or point in being picky
But the pink
Makes me ache as much as seeing her suffer
So for the last two months and the previous 54 years
She's been misplaced, displaced
In death mistreated almost as much as in life
I've sat with her as she suffered
And now it falls to me to carry on her suffering
It falls to me
Two months gone
To give her a proper burial

SO/STILL

no longer a Facebook friend of his
kicked to the curb
he'd finally had enough
was it something I said
I don't believe in optimism
you never talk to me anymore
I get it
a fit of anger/broken-heartedness
I de-friended him momentarily, weeks ago
I deleted his number and email
but I apologized, went so far as to re-friend him
so/still somehow I don't think I deserve his gesture of ill-
will
and besides I'm horny
got some new sex books and wanna try out what I've been
missing
in a fit of anger/indignation
I deleted Air Force John's number, months ago
he's no good
but I sure would like to cuddle
naked now

HOW TO REMAIN CLASSY IN UNCOMFORTABLE SITUATIONS

An incomplete list but generally:

- Let's say you trip in high school. No, let's say that you're ten years out of high school but visit a metropolitan school with, say, 2,000 students. Let's say you trip on a plank of wood that is in the middle of the hallway. Let's say you do not catch yourself in any way. Let's say that time slows down so that you can make eye contact with the hordes of people that are watching you plummet to the ground. A teacher says, concerned, "Are you okay?" and a student helps you up. You're embarrassed, but I mean, what are you going to do? It's okay that you don't look anyone in the eyes. It's okay your face is bright red. You should make like a champion, shake out your luminous hair, and say, "could you please tell me where the office is?"

- Let's say you met a great gal on a dating service, initiated contact, called her a few times, said you might be visiting her town on a certain day, and told her you'd give her a ring. And then, of course, you didn't. Then, let's say you see her on a different dating service and you decide you are going to do the right thing, shake out your luminous hair and send the following message: Too funny! I have thought about you several times. My life got kind of hectic and I knew I dropped the ball with our previous communications. I have thought about e-mailing you several times, but I guess was standoff-ish due to dropping off the face of the planet towards the end. I just joined here. How about you? I would love to hear back from you. Please accept my deepest apologies about before.

- Take lots of pain medication when in pain. And shake out your luminous hair.

- If you are walking on a hill outside of your local Olive Garden, trip, fall, and splatter your leftovers all over yourself and your gay escort, what you should do is stand up, regain as much dignity as the lasagna layers dripping off your being allows, shake out your luminous hair, and say, "Pretend you didn't just see that" to anyone who might've just seen that.

- If you demand a guy kiss you in a Wal-Mart parking lot who does not want to kiss you, shake your luminous hair out and get the hell away from your pathetic self and the awkward situation you just created.

- If your "friends" in high school notice your bald spot from when you were but a baby and ill and point it out to everyone who will listen at a pep rally, shake your luminous hair out, preferably covering up the bald spot and do not speak to so-called friends for a certain length of time. Remind them of this incident from time to time.

- In reference to your parents not knowing or caring about how or what they named you, tell your mother that if you have twins you are going to name them Sincere and Vengeful just to show them the slight they have done to you.

SURELY

a small growth, panic
cancer=hospice
hospice=slow death, sure death
Sure, death, sure.
Sure
death
sure cancer
small cancer
sure growth
panicky sureness
cancery sureness
deathly sureness
surely cancer
growth=sure

SUCH THINGS AS THIS

Inbox says (1) new message
Just then (2) new messages
My God, could it be
Usually not
Usually naught
Unusually knot
My love in a Sir Mix-a-Lot basket
Spare the spearhead
the spearmint
the spirit man
Inbox says nothing
I wait on the porch, old school

HEAT

there is a distinct smoggy air
between Mom and Dad
and me in the middle on
a hot, humid night at Grandma's
they're sleeping or pretending to
and I am
choking in the middle
the three of us all together
miserable
I would rather be alone in a strange place than
wedged between the two
with no air conditioning
and only the scent of sweat
and pee and mildew
amplified by the heat

DEAD ENDS

I told my stylist
Cut my hair
Get rid of the afterthoughts
The strays and the grays
Make me shine
I like to look new
Even if I'm used
All used up
Split ends that end up dead
Uneven lines and uneven psyches
Cut my hair
I told my stylist
To which he replied
Are you sure?

RANDOM LAUGHTER

This one
with the blond hair
the green eyes
easily burned skin
a writer of all words witty
shorter than my normal requirements
This one
who is at least as random as I am
talks in parallel circles around me
he makes me laugh
and it makes me laugh to think I might make him laugh

SHIT TO YOU AND YOURS

My dad said
Well
shit IS sticky
meaning it binds us
together

and so
I say to you
may you become close to those around you

may shit happen
to you
and yours

BY WAY OF OTHERS

What's true is 1979
1 + 9 + 7 + 9
is 26
is 8.
What's true is the table must be touched
1-2-3 times. And again.
What's true is if it's unclean, there's dirt. Dirt has
approximately
1 gazillion germs.
What's true is if I don't do what my mind says, it will
punish me
5,834 different ways
Which is 20
Which is 2
Which is true.

HOW HOWDY-DO RUINED MY LOVELIFE

what had happened was
a big misunderstanding
the cat scratch
the dog small
a reply misguided
inappropriately unquestioned by the sender
what could the receiver do
howdy
do

THE WOULD-HAVE-BEEN LIFE OF POPEYE

If Popeye had gone dating online
he wouldn't have had this trouble
accepting a woman who had a thing on the side
trust me, when the cameras weren't rolling, sweetest Olive
        was being pounded in the back of the soundstage by
        one mighty Brutus
After all, Popeye had a small dick
(It's true)
Popeye could have gotten a woman who would've gladly
settled for him,
his underperforming penis, his smoking and dental issues,
his eye patch
He could have been as big as Brutus, online
but he chose a canned spinach delusion
over outright lies and big hair

REAR-ENDED

I got it from behind
against my will
he was right
it was a rape
he didn't ask if I was okay
coldly stared at the reaction
to his sociopathic experiment
left as if an apparition
leaving me to swear
it happened

PROGNOSIS

Progress has been made
>when the color he loved doesn't automatically
>remind me of him

Progress when pea green can just be a pretty color
>again

Progress when lime doesn't force the echoes of
>*I have no affection to give you* to ring in my
>ears

Progress when I lay me down to sleep and can
>imagine tickling grass under my feet and not
>feel such loss

Progress when green doesn't make me see scarlet
>or black or anger or sadness but has instead
>returned to simply being green

NO GOD

No God
The license plate says
NGD
No God
I'll say
but maybe
I'm godless
today
because instead of narcotics
I am stuck
with over-the-counter.

THE RULES OF THE NOOSE

the saying
given enough rope
a man, my man, will hang himself
every time
applies

a concerted effort
give him lots of room to work
so that he has to struggle
to get a good grasp

overlook everything
and see him break and writhe
under the pressure
as the noose pulls tight
until at long last his eyes stare at you
dim and disbelieving

ANNIVERSARY

it was a year ago today
since I saw him last
it was a year ago yesterday
that he told me he had no affection for me
branded it into my psyche

it was a year ago yesterday
and on this anniversary
by coincidence only
he emailed me
wondered if we were on speaking terms

it was a year ago
I would have forgotten it was our anniversary
if he hadn't contacted me

it was a year ago
I cannot bring myself to believe
he's been counting, too

MARGINS

my thoughts lay dormant
for a couple of years
after her death
until one Wednesday in November
I found my cognitive baggage
confined to the margins around
my sudoku workbook
she's been left to rot,
I wrote the summer she was dying
What's left to rot now,
I wonder as I shrug the pages away,
watching them fall to trash,
with the same enthusiasm
as I shrugged her life away

TO MY DEAREST, PART 5

To: My Dearest
From: Medicated Lady

　　Re: Evaluation

There is compelling evidence that you do not feel you have made an error in judgment concerning me. This is disappointing as I had not terminated you; I had only put you on probation. I fully expected for you to come through a reassessment with no problems. However, it has come to my attention that you are refusing to return to your senses. Weeks gone by and now it seems you've redirected adoration toward another.

All possible scenarios have dwindled to a singular ray pointed at the Exit sign. It appears the fire alarm has been going off for some time now, everyone has left the building except me. It is strictly against company policy to leave me behind.

Since your resignation, I have considered your tenure with me. I contemplated what might be said if you were to realize your mistake.

- How dare you come back around after saying you were not ready for a relationship?
- How could you tell me you didn't want to have sex with me anymore because you wanted to look around? How could you not see I was a good thing, right in front of you? There was nothing to look around for.
- I hate you.
- I love you.
- Let's take things slow.
- Let's fuck.

It is as this point that I have to express my disappointment with your finagling with wig shopkeepers. I would be remiss if I did not mention that your deception in this matter has not improved your performance evaluation.

As you know, company policy states that evaluations are given regardless of manner of discharge: resignation or termination. In this case, you resigned before I was able to terminate you. This gives me pause. Since I cannot give your evaluation to you, I give it to the world. It is not favorable. I would hope that, though you are not officially required to do so, you would not shirk your responsibilities and give me the opportunity to say I never want to see you again. Should you do this, your performance rating would dramatically increase.

I hope that you will be able to reconsider your position and come back to me in the future. If only so I can fire you.

TECHNICAL REMOVAL OF RELATIONAL PROPORTIONS

has to be done,
the erasing, the deletion
from my hard drive,
my cell, my email,
it's the same
as the permanent tattoo
remover pen,
pretend it's not there,
the pain, and it's gone,
you're gone,
he's gone,
never was there,
never was there,
never was

NEED YOU

I need you to make me cry now
Don't speak to me
or call
or otherwise
anymore
Don't connect
in any way
so that I can disconnect
Just vanish
make me as invisible as I already I am

I need you to make me cry now
punish me
Rejuvenate the truth
don't let me pretend
or otherwise
anymore
I want to be destroyed now
devastated
so I can get on with it

I'VE CAUGHT SOMETHING

Not my dearest just yet.
a raccoon man, much older than he looks.
patrickshead, which is bald.
a casanova, a hotteach, a sexy4u or some such.
some other man, who caught me looking.

A boy younger with a cute smile.
A boy older with an edge and an attitude.
A boy with a nice body.

Now is the perfect time.
Now is perfection.

This whole time.
I thought I'd be witty.
and now I realize I'm just sad.

And when they leave me cold.
Only then.
they will be truly dear.

HOW TO KEEP A MAN

Hell if I know.

ANT

Last night,
I had a dream. A single

      ant

was scurrying up a white door frame,
and I knew
absolutely.
I have no idea what I knew,
but it was fulfilling and true
in an inexplicable way.

CARLEY

It's my friend and me
and her newborn
on a week night sometime in July.
The baby likes to be held
and really who doesn't.
Tonight she's fussy
but I appreciate her diva temper
as she screams and turns red in my arms
before falling fast asleep from exhaustion.
My friend and I take notice
but continue watching whatever we're watching
and talking about crazy siblings and extended family
members.
The baby wakes up
and promptly begins screaming
where she left off.
My friend and I talk over the racket
I admire a girl that won't let things go
and I know her spirit will serve her well.

ANOTHER BITTER END

So it's come to this, he says.
Guess so. My eyes dart away from his as if I can somehow escape the awkwardness.
I said I was sorry, he says. As if I am the one being difficult.
I look down. I hate confrontation. I think I might hedge.
So I say nothing.
The silence spreads out like glue, forever pasting us to this uncomfortable moment and each other.
He continues to gaze at me.
I don't know what you want me to say, I say. *I can't make you understand if you don't or you won't.*
I wonder, how many times I have uttered these words in the real world and in my head.
If you want me to forgive you, don't say you're sorry.
He looks at me, puzzled, dumbfounded, which I could've predicted all along.

PATIO GAS CAN

There's no symbolism on my patio.

There are pine needles covering the concrete.
A leg from one of the wrought iron chairs
has been left lying around.
The plants have wilted or died or lived.
My bike has not moved from where it was originally
positioned months ago.

Sitting atop my patio table, a red gas can has made itself
the centerpiece
by its color
and the way it looks as if it might be of use any moment.

And this is what my epiphany is.

Last summer, I ran out of gas.
He took me to the gas station, picked out the gas can for me
to buy, and filled the can with gas I bought.
The gas is long gone and so is he,
and this gas can is the lone, useful result of our union.
We had a gas can together.
That is all.

And this is what my epiphany is:
There's no symbolism on my patio.

POUTY BITCH

Inviting them to fuck
themselves is a virtue, Antigone
It's easy to bury a hero
much harder to bury the dog-dead

I can't imagine starving
to death is so bad, though
I'm sure you got really skinny
and as a woman, I could use
a little forced weight loss myself
I'm sure you might complain about it
but, honey, for the love of gods,
all you do is complain

The gods are fickle, Antigone
Your fatal flaw is being a pouty bitch
and there's not room
enough for that in this world
Still, you'd be an instant hit
as the token little woman
on Fox or MSNBC

WISHLESS

If I wished at all
I would not wish you well
I'd wish for hell
For you to burn
And turn fitful
In your waking and night dreams
I'd wish for your demise
That if you couldn't be happy with me
You couldn't be happy at all
I'd wish for your joy to be extinguished
Your life to be hollow and barren
Your days to be filled with endless time and questions
I'd wish you dead
On the inside
On the other side
Where I was forbidden to go
Cast out
I'd wish
If I wished at all

PROBLEMS WITH THIS POEM

There is no imagery.
It does not rhyme.
It has no rhythm.
It has complete thoughts and sentences.
It has punctuation.
There are inappropriate

line breaks that disrupt

the

flow.
It is not appropriately sunny or cheerful or
pretentious enough.

Also, this is not a poem.

I cannot call myself poet.
Except I do.

RIPE

no one to blame
winters are ripe for goodbyes
as the snow recedes
so do pleasantries
we get raw

another storm is coming
and it's going to be bad
winters fit me snugly
like a pencil skirt
encapsulating my confusion and loneliness
but at least
it's raw

BONES, LONG LINGERING

a dirt road with no name
known only by memory
no signs that say *this way*

it's been years since I visited your bones

in a field
under the stone
in the ground
above what remains
bones and your name
irrelevant dates
irrelevant days
because you're gone

in the graveyard of my bone and blood

fifty-six years
but only seven years, eight days with me

I haven't brought flowers
I can only offer sadness
long lingering

her stone awaits
already carved
ready for her life
to begin again with you

with melancholic and chronic love
your Kay-Kay
long lingering
forevermore

GOODBYE, LINCOLN NEBRASKA

Goodbye, Lincoln Nebraska
with your tall stalks of well-kept corn
a bright, flirty yellow
encouraging personification
and projection
on mindless plants

ABOUT THE AUTHOR

Loria Taylor lives in Little Rock, Arkansas, with her adopted dogs, ringtones, expired sliced turkey, and freckles. She has previously been published in *Literature and Medicine*, *Breadcrumb Scabs*, and *vox poetica*. *SOB* is her first book.

www.loriataylor.com

GRATITUDE

I am grateful to the many friends and family, bouts of depression, romps with mania, pit stops on the side of the road because I ran out of gas, the dating deluge of assholes, the shameless enjoyment of inappropriate jokes, the holy ritual of blood letting that made me sob and, thus, made *SOB* possible.

Also, thanks to my parents, who enjoy my quirks and have no memory of my being born. Thanks to Bryan, who cares for me when I pass out, blow up, break up, spew forth and then contractually obligates me to write about it.

Rumor has it I get more royalties if I say thank you to Sibling Rivalry Press for giving me an incredible opportunity. So, thank you for giving me an incredible opportunity.

Sob it out,

Loria
Your humble Medicated Lady

ABOUT THE PUBLISHER

The mission of Sibling Rivalry Press is to develop, publish, and promote outlaw artistic talent—those projects which inspire people to read, challenge, and ponder the complexities of life in dark rooms, under blankets by cell-phone illumination, in the backseats of cars, and on spring-day park benches next to people reading Plath and Atwood. We welcome manuscripts which push boundaries, sing sweetly, or inspire us to perform karaoke in drag. Not much makes us flinch.

For more information, visit us online.

www.siblingrivalrypress.com

www.ingramcontent.com/pod-product-compliance
Lightning Source LLC
LaVergne TN
LVHW091205080426
835509LV00006B/835